Trello a more comprehensive Guideline for beginners and advanced

Introduction to Trello

- What is Trello and how does it work?
- The benefits of Trello for project management and organization.

basics

- Set up a Trello account.
- Creating boards, lists and cards.
- Manage team members and permissions.

Effective use of maps

- Add description, checklists and comments.
- Use due dates and labels.
- Integrate attachments and power-ups.

Advanced Features

- Automation with Trello Butler.
- Using Trello for Agile Methods (Kanban).
- Customization of Trello with custom fields.

cooperation and teamwork

- Communicating and collaborating with team members.
- Integrating Trello with other tools (e.g. Slack, Google Drive).
  Trello Strategies:
- Best practices for organizing projects.
- Efficient use of labels, filters and search functions.
  Tips and Tricks:
- Keyboard shortcuts and time savers.
- Avoid mistakes and solve common problems.
  Trello on different platforms:
- Using Trello on desktop, mobile, and tablet.
  Trello Security:
- Protection of data and privacy.
- Account security recommendations.

Case studies and application examples

- How companies use Trello for different projects.
- Successful project management scenarios.

Summary

Introduction

Welcome to the comprehensive introduction to the versatile world of Trello - a powerful project management tool that helps companies and individuals to organize their tasks and projects efficiently, to keep track of them and to successfully implement them. In this comprehensive guide, we'll dive deep into the many ways Trello can be used for different scenarios and project types. From software development to marketing campaigns, event management, product development to customer support, Trello offers the flexibility to thrive in a wide range of business and personal situations. Also, we will cover important aspects like account security, privacy, best practices and efficient usage techniques to get the most out of this powerful tool

introduction
Trello for beginners
and
advanced

Welcome to our comprehensive book on Trello—a powerful project management and team collaboration platform! Whether you're just getting started with Trello or already have experience with the software, this book provides you with a solid introduction and plenty of advanced tips for unleashing Trello's full potential.

In today's fast-paced world, effective organization and collaboration is essential, whether for personal projects or company-wide initiatives. Trello empowers you to navigate the chaos of everyday life by providing intuitive boards, lists, and cards that provide a clear structure for your ideas, tasks, and goals.

Part 1: Basics and Getting Started We'll start with the basics and walk you through setting up your Trello account. You will learn how to create boards, lists and cards while making the best use of the various functions. So you are well prepared to organize your projects and keep track of them.

Part 2: Using Cards Effectively and Advanced Features Discover the variety of possibilities that Trello cards offer. From creating checklists to using due dates and labels, we'll show you how to make your work more efficient. We'll also cover advanced features like automation with Trello Butler and using Trello for Agile methods.

Part 3: Collaboration and Teamwork Successful projects require seamless team collaboration. In this section, you'll learn how to communicate with team members, share files, and integrate Trello with other tools. Together you can work effectively on projects and increase your productivity.

Part 4: Trello strategies and expert tips Use proven strategies to keep your boards and cards organized. We share expert tips on using labels, filters, and search features to make your projects even more effective. You will also learn how to adapt Trello to your individual needs by using custom fields.

Part 5: Trello on Different Platforms and Security Learn how to use Trello efficiently on desktop, mobile, and tablet. We give you advice on how to protect your data and ensure your privacy. Safety is paramount when it comes to using Trello.

Part 6: Case Studies and Use Cases We let you be inspired by successful case studies and show you how companies and teams use Trello for different projects. The practical application examples illustrate how versatile Trello can be used for a wide variety of scenarios.

Whether you use Trello for personal tasks, a team project, or to manage an entire company, this e-book will accompany you on your journey and give you valuable knowledge to get the most out of Trello. So, let's dive into the world of efficient project organization together and take your productivity to a new level!

introduction
in
Trello

What is Trello and how does it work

Trello is a powerful web-based project management and collaboration platform that empowers individuals and teams to manage tasks, projects, and ideas in a visual and organized way. Developed by Fog Creek Software in 2011, Trello quickly became one of the most popular collaboration tools for everything from small teams to large enterprises.

The basic principle of Trello: The kanban board Trello is based on the concept of the kanban board, which was originally developed in production planning. A Kanban board consists of horizontal columns called "lists" and vertical cards representing each task, also called "cards". Each card represents a specific task or idea and can be moved around the different lists to show its current status.

Boards, lists and cards: Trello boards are the main workspaces where projects and tasks are organized. You can create multiple boards to manage different projects or tasks.

On a Trello board, you create lists that can represent different phases of a project, workflow statuses, or categories. Examples of lists could be To-Do, In Progress, Completed, or Ideas.

The actual tasks or ideas are placed on the lists in the form of cards. These cards contain information and details about the task at hand.

You can add descriptions, checklists, due dates, attachments, and more to cards to capture all the important information.

How Trello works: Drag-and-drop and flexibility Trello is characterized by its simple and intuitive user interface. You can simply drag and drop cards between lists to change the status of tasks. This makes it easy to track progress and see the current status of a project at a glance.

Trello's flexibility allows you to customize the platform to meet your unique needs. You can create new lists and cards, rename or delete existing ones, add colors and labels, and much more. Trello also offers the ability to integrate Power-Ups, which provide additional functionality and integrations with other tools to further increase productivity.

Collaboration and communication: Trello supports real-time collaboration. You can invite team members to your boards and give them specific permissions to collaborate on projects. Comments can be left directly on the cards to start discussions, ask questions or share updates.

The integration: Trello is also known for its seamless integration with other tools. You can connect Trello to platforms like Slack, Google Drive, Dropbox, GitHub, and many others to seamlessly share and sync information and files.

Overall, Trello is a powerful and flexible platform that allows individuals and teams to organize their projects and tasks in a visually appealing and structured format. The visual nature of the Kanban board makes the work more transparent and helps everyone involved to keep track and collaborate efficiently. Whether you're a project planner, team leader, freelancer, or creative mind, Trello gives you the tools to be more productive and thrive.

The benefits of Trello for project management and organization

Trello offers numerous project management and organizational benefits that make it a popular and effective tool for individuals and teams. Here are the in-depth benefits of Trello:

1. Visual Organization: Trello uses the Kanban board system, which provides a visual and intuitive way to organize tasks and projects. By clearly presenting lists and cards on one board, you can keep track of the progress and status of each task. The visual design makes it easy to understand the progress of the project and facilitates team collaboration.

2. Flexibility and customization: Trello adapts to the unique needs of each user. You can create, rename and arrange boards, lists and cards however you like. You can also use colors, labels, and custom fields to improve the structure and visibility of your tasks. Trello's flexible nature allows you to use it for different project types and work processes.

3. Easy task management: Trello makes it easy to create, move, and prioritize tasks. New tasks are simply created as cards on a matching list and can then be dragged and dropped between lists to update their status. This makes it easier to delegate tasks and keep everyone involved in the loop.

4. Transparent cooperation: Trello encourages team collaboration by enabling real-time collaboration. Team members can comment on each other's cards and boards, share files, and provide feedback. This allows team members to communicate effectively, share ideas, and solve problems without having to resort to different communication platforms.

5. Efficient Project Tracking: Trello makes it easy to track the progress of a project. By moving cards from one list to the next, you can see how tasks are progressing and where bottlenecks are occurring. This helps identify potential delays early and take action to complete projects on time.

6. Project overview and prioritization: The ability to capture all relevant information about a task in one card gives you a comprehensive overview of the entire project. The visual representation helps prioritize tasks and identify critical milestones to increase productivity and streamline project execution.

7. Integrations with other tools: Trello offers integrations with a variety of other tools and services like Slack, Google Drive, Jira, GitHub, and more. This allows you to seamlessly sync data and files between different platforms and further improve information sharing.

8. Flexible use in different areas: Trello can be used in various fields and industries, be it for software development, marketing campaigns, event planning, personal to-do lists or managing complex projects. Trello's adaptability allows it to be tailored to the specific needs of each project or team.

9. Mobility and Accessibility: Trello is web-based and also offers apps for different platforms like iOS and Android. This allows users to access and work on their projects from anywhere in the world. The ability to use Trello on desktops, laptops, tablets, and smartphones makes it a flexible tool for those on the go or working remotely.

Overall, Trello offers a user-friendly and efficient solution for project management and organization. Its visual presentation, transparent collaboration, and customization make it a popular choice for individuals and teams looking to increase productivity and successfully complete projects.

The basics

Set up a Trello account

Setting up a Trello account is a simple process and only takes a few minutes. Here is a detailed step-by-step guide:

Step 1: Go to the Trello website Open your favorite web browser and go to the official Trello website: https://trello.com/

Step 2: Sign up for a new account Click Sign Up or Sign In, depending on which option is currently displayed on the site. If you don't have an existing Trello account, select Sign Up.

Step 3: Fill in the registration form A registration form opens in which you have to enter your personal data. Fill out the required fields:

- Name: Enter your first and last name.
- Email address: Use a valid email address that you use regularly.
- Password: Choose a secure password made up of letters, numbers, and special characters. Make sure it's not easy to guess.

Step 4: Confirm Account Creation Once you have entered all the required information, click the "Register" or similar button. Trello sends a confirmation email to the email address you provided.

Step 5: Email verification Go to your email inbox and look for the verification email from Trello. Open the email and click on the confirmation link it contains. This will verify your email address and activate your Trello account.

Step 6: Get started with Trello After you've verified your email address, you'll be taken to your Trello dashboard. Here you can create your first board and start organizing your tasks.

Optional: You can also download the Trello apps for iOS or Android on your smartphone or tablet. Just go to the App Store (iOS) or Google Play Store (Android) and search for "Trello". Download the official Trello app and sign in with your previously created credentials to use Trello on mobile.

Congratulations! You've now successfully created a Trello account and can organize your projects, tasks, and ideas on Trello boards. Trello's simple and intuitive interface lets you collaborate efficiently with team members and increase your productivity. Have fun discovering the diverse functions and possibilities that Trello offers!

Creating boards, lists and cards

Creating boards, lists, and cards in Trello is an important step in organizing your projects and tasks. Here's a detailed guide on how to do this in Trello:

Step 1: Sign in to Trello Open your web browser and go to the Trello website: https://trello.com/ If you are not already logged in, log in with your previously created login data (email address and password).

Step 2: View the Dashboard After you sign in, you'll be taken to the Trello dashboard. Here you will find an overview of all your boards and teams.

Step 3: Create a new board Click on the "Create" button, which is usually located at the top right of the dashboard. Select the "Board" option from the drop down menu.

Step 4: Board Title and Description Give your board a meaningful name that describes the project or tasks you want to organize on it. You can also add an optional description to further explain the board. Then click "Create" to create the board.

Step 5: Creating Lists After you create the board, it will appear on your dashboard. Now you can create lists to represent the different phases or categories of your project. By default, a board is created with a list called "To-Do".

Click the "Add List" button located at the bottom right of the board. Enter the name of the list and press Enter. Repeat this process to add more lists. Examples of lists could be: "In progress", "Completed", "Awaiting feedback", etc.

Step 6: Creating Cards Now you can create cards to represent individual tasks or ideas that you want to organize in the lists. Click on the list where you want to create a new card.

Type in the title of the card and press Enter. This creates the map. You can then open the map to add more information, such as: B. a detailed description, checklists, due dates, attachments and much more.

Step 7: Moving cards between lists You can simply drag and drop cards from one list to another to update their status or progress. This makes it easy to move tasks from one stage to the next as they are edited or completed.

Congratulations! You've successfully created a new Trello board, added lists, and start creating Trello by adding more details about your cards, inviting team members, and exploring the many other features Trello offers. Good luck with organizing and managing your projects!

Manage team members and permissions

Managing team members and permissions in Trello is an essential part of collaboration and allows tasks and projects to be efficiently organized as a team. Here's a detailed guide on how to invite team members and manage their permissions in Trello:

Step 1: Accessing the Board Team Menu Open the Trello board where you want to add team members and manage their permissions. Then click on the "More" button (three dots) in the top-right area of the board and select the "Team Settings" option from the drop-down menu.

Step 2: Add Team Members In the Team Settings menu you will find a section called "Add Members". Enter the email addresses of the people you want to invite as team members. If they already have Trello accounts, they are automatically added to the team. If not, they'll receive an invitation email to sign up for Trello and join the team.

Step 3: Manage Permissions After you've added team members, you can adjust their permissions to control access to the board.

You have three main options:

- Team Members: They have full access to the board and can create, edit, move and delete cards and do all other activities.
- Observer: You can view the board and comment on cards, but don't have editing rights.
- Disabled: You have no access to the board.

Step 4: Individual Card Permissions (Optional) In addition to team member permissions, you can also set individual permissions for specific team members on specific cards. Click on a card in the board to open it. Then click the "More" button (three dots) in the top right corner of the card and select "Permissions" from the drop-down menu. Here you can set the permissions for this specific team member, independent of the general team member permissions.

Step 5: Team management As a board owner or team admin, you have the ability to remove team members, change their permissions, or leave the team. To do this, go to the team settings again and navigate to the "Members" section.

A notice: If you're working in a free Trello account, team management options may be more limited than in a Trello Business Class or Enterprise account.

With these steps, you can invite team members to your Trello board, manage their permissions, and ensure all team members have appropriate access to collaborate effectively on projects and tasks. Clear management of permissions helps ensure security and privacy, and ensure all team members are on the same page.

effective use
from
Map

Add description, checklists and comments

In Trello, you can add descriptions, checklists, and comments to cards to capture additional information about a task or project and improve communication with team members. Here is a detailed guide to each of these features:

1. Add descriptions: Descriptions are a way to add important information and details to a map. You can write a description to explain the content or goal of the task, provide instructions, or share important information.

Step 1: Open the Trello board that has the card you want to add a description to.

Step 2: Click on the map to open it.

Step 3: Click on the text box below the card's title. Here you can enter your description.

Step 4: Once you've written the description, click outside the text box or press Enter to save the description.

2. Add checklists: Checklists are a great way to break tasks down into smaller, manageable steps and track progress.

Step 1: Open the card you want to add a checklist to.

Step 2: Click the "Add Checklist" button.

Step 3: Enter a name for the checklist and press Enter to create it.

Step 4: Now you can add individual tasks or steps to the checklist by clicking on the text box below the checklist.

Step 5: When you've completed a task step, you can click the checkbox next to it to mark it as complete.

3. Add Comments: Comments allow you and your teammates to exchange views on a map, ask questions, or share updates.

Step 1: Open the card you want to add a comment to.

Step 2: Scroll down to the Comments section.

Step 3: Click on the text box below the existing comments to enter your own comment.

Step 4: Click outside the text box or press Enter to post your comment.

A notice: Descriptions, checklists, and comments are extremely useful for collaborating with team members. Team members can read the descriptions to improve understanding of the map, use the checklist to track task progress, and use comments to clarify questions and provide feedback. By using these features, communication becomes more efficient and everyone involved can work together in a more informed and coordinated manner.

Use due dates and labels

In Trello, you can use due dates and labels to better organize your tasks and projects and keep track of important dates. Here's a detailed guide on how to use due dates and labels in Trello:

1. Add due dates: Due dates are useful for tying tasks or projects to specific dates and ensuring important deadlines are met.

Step 1: Open the Trello board and the card you want to add a due date to.

Step 2: Click on the calendar icon in the card to add the due date.

Step 3: Select the desired date from the calendar by clicking on it. You can also manually edit the field and enter the date.

Step 4: Click outside the calendar or press Enter to save the due date.

Step 5: After you add the due date, it will appear on the card. You can also sort the card by due dates to prioritize the tasks with the most pressing deadlines.

2. Use labels: Labels are colored markers you can add to cards to categorize, organize, or prioritize tasks.

Step 1: Open the map you want to add a label to.

Step 2: Click on the "Label" button in the right sidebar of the map.

Step 3:A drop-down menu will appear with a list of available labels. Click on the label you want to add or select "Create New Label" to create a new label with a custom color.

Step 4: Click outside the drop-down menu to save the label to the map.

Step 5: You can add multiple labels to a card simply by clicking the label icon and selecting more labels.

A notice: Due dates and labels help you keep track of and prioritize your tasks and projects. You can use due dates to ensure important tasks get done on time and use labels to group tasks by topic, responsibility, or priority. By using these features in Trello, you can increase your productivity and organize your work more efficiently.

Integrate attachments and power-ups

1. Add attachments in Trello: Attachments allow you to upload files, images, or documents directly to Trello cards and link them to your tasks and projects. This is especially useful when you want to share files with team members or attach important reference materials for a task.

Step 1: Open the Trello card you want to add an attachment to.

Step 2: Click on the "Attachment" button in the map view. A window will appear allowing you to upload files from your computer or cloud storage.

Step 3: Select the files you want and click "Open" (or "Upload" depending on your operating system).

Step 4: The selected files are now shown in the map and are visible to all team members. You can click on the files to download or open them.

2. Integrate Power-Ups into Trello: Power-Ups are extensions that allow adding additional features and integrations to Trello. Power-Ups extend Trello's functionality by adding features like calendar views, time tracking, automatic actions, and more.

Step 1: Open the Trello board you want to add a power-up to.

Step 2: Click on the "More" button (three dots) in the top right area of the board and select the "Power-Ups" option from the drop-down menu.

Step 3:A window will open showing a list of available power-ups.

Step 4: Search for the power-up you want by either scrolling through the list or typing the name of the power-up in the search box.

Step 5: Click on the power-up you want to add. Another window will open with more information about the power-up.

Step 6: Click on the "Add" button to add the power-up to your board.

Step 7: After adding the power-up, it will appear in the right sidebar of the board. You can click on the power-up to configure it and take advantage of the additional features it offers.

A notice: Attachments and power-ups are great ways to customize Trello to your specific needs and increase productivity. Attachments let you upload files directly into Trello and link them to your tasks, while Power-Ups add additional features and integrations to make Trello even more powerful. By using these features, you can get the most out of Trello for the way you work and projects, and further improve your efficiency.

advanced
functions

Automation with Trello Butler

Trello Butler is a powerful automation tool for Trello that makes it possible to automate repetitive tasks and simplify complex workflows. Butler lets you create custom actions to automatically manage cards and boards once certain conditions are met. Here is a detailed guide on how to use Trello Butler:

1. Activate Butler: Before you can use Trello Butler, you must first enable it on your Trello board. To do this, go to the board you want to use Butler on.

Step 1: Click the "More" button (three dots) in the top-right area of the board and select "Automation" from the drop-down menu.

Step 2: Click Activate Butler. This will enable Butler for the board and the Butler toolbar will appear in the right sidebar.

2. Set up triggers and actions: Trello Butler lets you set triggers and actions to trigger specific actions when certain conditions are met. There are two main types of triggers, "When a card is created" and "When an appointment is added". The possible actions are extensive and can be adjusted as required.

Step 1: Click on the Butler toolbar in the right sidebar to open the Butler pop-up window.

Step 2: Click "Add Custom Action" to create a new automation.

Step 3: Choose a trigger from the list of available trigger types.

Step 4: Select one or more conditions that must be met for the trigger to fire. For example, you can specify that the trigger runs only for specific cards, labels, lists, or team members.

Step 5: Choose one or more actions to take when the trigger fires. Actions can be moving cards, adding comments, changing due dates, assigning team members, and more.

Step 6: Configure the actions according to your needs. You can personalize the actions with text templates, variables and custom options.

Step 7: Click "Create" to set up the automation.

3. Manage Butler Rules: After you create an automation with Butler, you can manage it from the Butler toolbar. You can edit, disable, or delete automations by clicking the gear icon next to the rule.

A notice: Trello Butler is a powerful tool that can boost productivity in Trello tremendously. With Butler, you can automate time-consuming manual tasks and streamline workflows so you can focus on what matters most. By cleverly using triggers and actions, you can simplify complex processes in Trello and get the most out of this great automation tool.

Using Trello for Agile Methods (Kanban)

Trello is an excellent platform to support agile methods like Kanban and to make project management more efficient. Kanban is an agile method that aims to visualize workflow, encourage team collaboration and improve continuous workflow. Here is a detailed guide on how to use Trello for agile Kanban methods:

1. Create a Kanban board: Open Trello and create a new board for your project. The board acts as a virtual whiteboard where you create your Kanban boards and organize tasks visually.

2. Define the work steps (lists): Create lists on your board to represent the different steps or phases of the project. Typical lists on a Kanban board are "To-Do", "In Progress", "Completed", etc.

3. Create cards for tasks: Create a separate card on the board for each task or project. Each card represents an independent entity that moves from one work step to the next.

4. Move cards through the lists: Use drag-and-drop to move cards between lists when a task's status changes. Start a card in the "To-Do" list, then drag it to the "In progress" list when you start it and finally to the "Completed" list when you complete the task.

5. Use labels for categorization: Use labels to categorize cards, for example by priority, responsibility or project type. Labels help to keep track and identify tasks that have certain characteristics in common.

6. Use due dates for deadlines: Add due dates to cards to mark important dates and deadlines. This allows you to keep track of progress and ensure tasks are completed on time.

7. Add task checklists: Add checklists to cards to break complex tasks down into smaller steps. This allows you to track progress within a task and ensure all steps are completed.

8. Use power-ups for advanced functions: Integrate power-ups to add additional functionality to your Kanban board. Power-Ups offer calendar views, time tracking, integrations with other tools, and more.

9. Use automations with Trello Butler: Use Trello Butler to automate repetitive tasks and simplify complex workflows. Create custom actions that are triggered when certain conditions are met.

10. Encourage team collaboration: Invite team members to your board so they can work on tasks together. Use comments to provide feedback and share progress.

By using Trello for agile Kanban methods, you can increase productivity, streamline workflow, and improve project management transparency. The visual representation of tasks on the board allows the team to see the status of work at a glance and identify problems early. Trello offers the flexibility and adaptability that are essential for implementing agile methods and supports you in organizing your projects efficiently and completing them successfully.

Customization of Trello with custom fields

Customizing Trello with custom fields is a powerful feature that allows you to add additional information to cards and customize Trello to your specific needs. Custom fields allow you to capture tailored information relevant to your projects or workflow. Here is a detailed guide on using custom fields in Trello:

1. Enable Custom Fields: Before you can use custom fields in Trello, you need to make sure your board has this feature enabled. Note that this feature is only available in Trello Business Class or Enterprise accounts.

Step 1: Open the Trello board where you want to add custom fields.

Step 2: Click on the "More" button (three dots) in the top-right area of the board and select "Settings" from the drop-down menu.

Step 3: In the board settings you will find the "Custom Fields" section. Click "Enable Custom Fields" to enable this feature.

2. Create custom fields: After you enable custom fields, you can create your own fields to add additional information to cards.

Step 1: Click the "More" button (three dots) again and select "Custom Fields" from the drop-down menu.

Step 2: Click "Add Field" to create a new custom field.

Step 3: Choose a field type for the custom field. You can choose between text, number, date and selection list.

Step 4: Enter a name for the custom field and add any additional options (e.g. picklist options) if you wish.

Step 5: Click "Add" to create the custom field.

3. Use custom fields in cards: Now you can add custom fields in cards to record additional information.

Step 1: Open the card you want to add a custom field to.

Step 2: Click the Fields button in the right sidebar.

Step 3: Select the custom field from the list and enter the appropriate value for the field.

Step 4: The input is saved automatically and is visible on the map.

4. Manage Custom Fields: You can edit, rename, or delete custom fields in the board settings as needs change.

A notice: Custom fields in Trello provide a powerful way to add additional information to cards and customize Trello to your unique needs. Whether it's project metrics, categorization or specific e optimal management of your projects and tasks.

Cooperation
and
Teamwork

Communicating and collaborating with team members

Communicating and collaborating with team members are critical to the success of projects. Trello offers several features to help you communicate effectively with your team and collaborate on tasks.

Here's a detailed guide on how to use Trello to communicate and collaborate with team members:

1. Inviting Team Members: To collaborate with teammates in Trello, you need to invite them to your board.

Step 1: Open the Trello board you're working on.

Step 2: Click on the "More" button (three dots) in the top-right area of the board and select "Team Settings" from the drop-down menu.

Step 3: Go to the "Add Members" section and enter the email addresses of the team members you want to invite. If they already have a Trello account, they are automatically added to the board. Otherwise, they'll receive an invitation email to sign up for Trello and join the board.

2. Comments and Discussions: Trello allows team members to add comments to cards to ask questions, provide feedback, or share updates.

Step 1: Open the card you want to add a comment to.

Step 2: Scroll down to the Comments section.

Step 3: Click on the text box below the existing comments to enter your own comment.

Step 4: Click outside the text box or press Enter to post your comment.

3. Assignment of Team Members: You can assign team members to cards to clearly establish ownership and accountability for tasks.

Step 1: Open the card you want to assign to a team member.

Step 2: Click on the "Members" button in the right sidebar.

Step 3: Select the team member from the list or add an email address to invite a new team member.

Step 4: The assigned team member is now displayed on the map.

4. Use of checklists: Use checklists in cards to break down complex tasks into smaller steps. Team members can track progress within the task.

Step 1: Open the card you want to add a checklist to.

Step 2: Click the "Add Checklist" button.

Step 3: Enter a name for the checklist and press Enter to create it.

Step 4: Add tasks to the checklist by clicking on the text box below the checklist.

Step 5: Click the checkbox next to each completed task to mark it.

5. Using Power-Ups and Integrations: Integrate power-ups and external tools to further improve collaboration with team members. Power-Ups offer features like time tracking, calendar views, file integrations and more.

A notice: Effective communication and collaboration with team members are critical to the smooth running of projects. By using Trello you can give feedback, clarify questions and make the progress of the team transparent. By using the features above, you can ensure that all team members are on the same page and can work efficiently together on tasks. Trello gives you the tools to optimize and successfully complete collaboration in your team.

Integrating Trello with other tools (e.g. Slack, Google Drive)

Trello's integration with other tools like Slack and Google Drive enables seamless collaboration and improves the efficiency of your workflows. Here's a detailed guide on how to integrate Trello with Slack and Google Drive:

1. Integration of Trello with Slack: Trello and Slack can be linked to share updates from Trello to Slack channels and vice versa. This allows team members to get information without leaving Trello or Slack.

Step 1: Open the Trello board you want to connect to Slack.

Step 2: Click on the "More" button (three dots) in the top-right area of the board and select "Settings" from the drop-down menu.

Step 3: Go to the Integrations section and search for Slack.

Step 4: Click "Connect to Slack" and follow the instructions to authorize the integration.

Step 5: Once connected, you can choose which Slack channel to share Trello updates to.

Step 6: Select the events to post to Slack, such as B. new cards, comments or changes in due dates.

Step 7: Click "Save" to complete the integration.

2. Integration of Trello with Google Drive: Trello and Google Drive can be linked to link files from Google Drive directly to Trello cards and vice versa. This gives you instant access to relevant files at all times.

Step 1: Open the Trello card you want to add a file from Google Drive to.

Step 2: Click on the "Attachment" button in the map view.

Step 3: Select "Google Drive" from the attachment options.

Step 4: You'll be prompted to sign in to your Google account if you haven't already.

Step 5: Find and select the file you want to attach.

Step 6: The file is now displayed in the map and is visible to all team members.

3. Integration with other tools: Trello also offers integrations with many other popular tools, such as B. Dropbox, Microsoft Teams, Evernote and more. These integrations extend Trello's functionality and allow it to work seamlessly with your favorite tools.

A notice: The integration of Trello with other tools opens up new possibilities for collaboration and makes it easier to access important information. By integrating with Slack, you can automatically share Trello updates to your Slack channels, keeping the team in the loop. With Google Drive integration, you can link files directly in Trello cards, creating a central location for all relevant information. Integration with other tools allows you to adapt Trello to the way you work and increase your team's productivity.

Best practices for organizing projects

The organization of projects is crucial to the success and efficiency in completing tasks. Here are detailed best practices for successfully organizing projects with Trello:

1. Create clear and concise boards: Start each project with its own Trello board. Give the board a meaningful name and use lists to structure the individual work steps or project phases. Use labels to categorize the cards and due dates to mark important dates.

2. Define clear tasks in cards: Create a separate card for each task or project. Formulate clear task descriptions and use checklists to break down complex tasks into manageable steps. Assign team members to establish ownership.

3. Use custom fields: Use custom fields to add additional information to maps relevant to your project. For example, custom fields could contain budget information, priorities, or project status.

4. Use checklists and power-ups: Checklists help you track progress within a task. Use power-ups to add additional features like calendar views, time tracking, or integrations with other tools.

5. Keep the board up to date: Keep the board up to date by moving cards to the appropriate lists, adding comments, and updating due dates. Periodically use filters to archive or remove obsolete or completed tasks.

6. Encourage team collaboration: Invite team members to your board and encourage collaboration by providing feedback, clarifying questions, and discussing progress. Use the integration with Slack to share real-time updates.

7. Prioritize tasks: Set priorities to get the most important tasks done first. Use labels or custom fields to indicate the urgency and importance of tasks.

8. Use templates: Create project templates to start recurring projects or tasks faster. Use Trello board templates or create your own to save time and ensure consistency.

9. Keep the board clean: Avoid too many lists or overloaded maps. Keep the board clean and organized so team members can easily access the information they need.

10. Evaluate and optimize: After completion of a project or phase, evaluate the process and the results. Use this experience to optimize future projects and establish best practices.

A notice: The successful organization of projects with Trello requires clear structures, transparent communication and careful planning. By applying the best practices above, you can get the most out of Trello to efficiently manage projects, encourage collaboration, and improve project outcomes. Good organization with Trello allows you and your team to keep track and complete projects successfully.

Efficient use of labels, filters and search functions

The efficient use of labels, filters and search functions in Trello helps to keep track of projects, find relevant information and streamline the workflow. Here are in-depth tips on how to get the most out of these features:

1. Labels: Labels are colored markers applied to cards to categorize them or to emphasize certain properties. To use labels efficiently:

- Create consistent color coding: Determine within the team which colors should be used for which categories or priorities in order to have a consistent system.
- Limit the number of labels: Avoid too many labels to keep the board uncluttered. Limit them to the most used categories.
- Use labels wisely: Use labels to mark important information, such as B. Priority, responsibility or project type.

2. Filter: Trello offers powerful filtering options to focus on relevant

information. Here are some tips for using filters efficiently:

- Use pre-made filters: Use the pre-made filter options like "My Cards" or "Due Dates" to show cards based on specific criteria.
- Create Custom Filters: Create custom filters to match specific search criteria. For example, you could create filters to show cards based on labels or responsibilities.
- Combine filters: Use multiple filters at the same time to get precise results. For example, combine filters for a specific label and assignee to show exactly the cards you need.

3. Search functions: Trello has a powerful search feature to quickly

find specific cards or content. Here are some tips for using the

search function efficiently:

- Use tags: Enter tags or keywords in the search bar to search for specific cards, labels, or content.
- Use search operators: Use search operators like quotation marks to search for exact phrases, or "OR" to search for results containing one of several keywords.
- Refine the search with filters: Use the search function in combination with filters to get specific results.

A notice: Through the efficient use of labels, filters and search

functions in Trello you can streamline the workflow and keep track

of projects. Using clear and consistent labels helps categorize cards

and highlight important information. Filters allow you to search for specific cards and focus on relevant tasks. The search feature provides a quick way to search for specific cards or content, increasing efficiency when working with Trello.

Keyboard shortcuts and time savers

Using keyboard shortcuts and time-savers in Trello can greatly increase efficiency and make navigating and editing boards, lists, and cards faster. Here are in-depth tips on how to make the most of keyboard shortcuts and time-savers:

1. Keyboard shortcuts for board navigation: Trello provides some handy keyboard shortcuts to quickly navigate between boards, lists, and cards:

- Switch boards: Press "b" followed by the Tab key to switch between boards.
- List switching: Press "l" followed by the Tab key to switch between lists.
- Map switching: Press "c" followed by the Tab key to switch between maps.

2. Fast Map Creation: To create a quick map without leaving the current board, use the following keyboard shortcuts:

- Press "n" followed by the Tab key to create a new card in the current list.
- Press "q" followed by the tab key to create a new card at the top of the current list.

3. Fast editing of cards: There are several keyboard shortcuts to edit maps quickly:

- Open the card you want to edit and press "e" to edit the card's title.
- Press "d" to edit the card's due date.
- Press "m" to add or remove teammates from the map.
- Press "l" to add or remove labels from the map.

4. Keyboard shortcuts in map views: When you are in a map you can use the following keyboard shortcuts:

- Press "r" to add a comment to the map.
- Press "t" to add a checklist in the map.

5. Use edit mode: Edit mode allows you to edit maps without using the mouse. Open the card you want to edit and press "Enter" to enter edit mode. You can then use the keyboard to edit the title, descriptions, or checklists.

6. **Save time with keyboard shortcuts:**Using keyboard shortcuts instead of the mouse allows you to navigate Trello and perform actions faster. This can be especially useful if you frequently switch between different boards, lists, and cards, or have to edit a lot of cards.

A notice: By using keyboard shortcuts and time savers, you can significantly increase productivity when working with Trello. Navigate between boards, lists, and cards, create new cards, and edit existing cards faster with these simple keyboard shortcuts. By using keyboard shortcuts effectively, you can streamline the workflow in Trello and spend more time actually working on your projects.

Avoid mistakes and solve common problems

When using Trello, errors can occur or common problems can arise. Here are detailed tips on how to avoid these mistakes and solve problems effectively:

1. Error: unclear structure and list overload:

- Solution: Make sure the board structure is clear and concise. Do not use too many lists, but select the necessary work steps or project phases. Think about what information you want to display on the board and use labels and custom fields to categorize the cards and highlight important details.

2. Error: Incomplete or unclear maps:

- Solution: Write clear task descriptions in the cards so team members know exactly what needs to be done. Use checklists to break down complex tasks into manageable steps. Assign team members to cards to establish ownership.

3. Mistake: Lack of communication in the team:

- Solution: Encourage team communication by using comments in cards to ask questions, give feedback, or share updates. Integrate Trello with Slack to share real-time updates and facilitate collaboration.

4th Mistake: Overuse of Keyboard Shortcuts and Filters:

- Solution: Although keyboard shortcuts and filters can increase efficiency, overuse can lead to confusion. Use keyboard shortcuts and filters when they're really useful, but stick to using the mouse in other cases to avoid confusion.

5. Problem: Loss of maps or information:

- Solution: Make sure your cards are saved and archived regularly to avoid losing information. If you accidentally delete maps or information, you can often restore them in the archive.

6. Problem: Missing notifications and due dates:

- Solution: Check your notifications and due dates regularly to make sure you don't miss any important updates or tasks. You can customize notification settings to only receive relevant information.

7. Problem: Conflicts when working together:

- Solution: Clarify responsibilities and communication channels in the team to avoid conflicts. Use comments to clear up misunderstandings and define clear responsibilities.

8. Problem: Too many open tasks:

- Solution: Prioritize tasks and work on one task at a time to avoid overload. Archive completed tasks to keep the board clutter-free.

9. Problem: Lack of data security:

- Solution: Make sure sensitive information is kept safe in Trello. If needed, use Trello Business Class or Enterprise accounts with additional security features. Make sure that access permissions are only granted to authorized team members.

A notice: Avoiding mistakes and solving common problems in Trello requires careful planning, clear communication, and regular workflow reviews. By considering the above tips and solutions, you can increase efficiency when using Trello and ensure smooth project management. Be proactive in resolving issues and liaise closely with your team to achieve the best results.

Using Trello on desktop, mobile, and tablet

Using Trello on multiple devices, including desktop, mobile, and tablet, gives you the flexibility to manage your projects and tasks from anywhere. Here are in-depth tips on how to use Trello effectively on different platforms:

1. Trello on desktop: The desktop version of Trello offers a rich and clean interface that allows you to see your boards, lists, and cards full-size. Here are some tips for using Trello effectively on desktop:

- Use keyboard shortcuts: Use keyboard shortcuts to quickly navigate between boards, lists, and cards, create new cards, or edit existing cards.
- Multitasking: Since the desktop offers more screen space, you can have multiple boards and maps open at the same time to work efficiently.
- Use integrations: You can easily use integrations like Google Drive or Slack to work seamlessly with other tools and share files or updates.

2. Trello on mobile devices (smartphones): The Trello mobile app allows you to stay productive and manage projects on the go. Here are some tips for using Trello effectively on mobile:

- Manage notifications: Adjust notification settings to only receive relevant updates and avoid notification overload.
- Swipe Gestures: Use swipe gestures to quickly switch between boards and cards, or perform actions like moving cards.
- Make cards on the go: Use the quick card making features to jot down ideas or tasks as they come to mind.
- Compact list view: If you have a lot of lists, switch to compact list view to see more information on one screen.

3. Trello on tablets: Trello on tablets offers a mix of the desktop and mobile experience and is ideal for medium-sized workers. Here are some tips for using Trello effectively on tablets:

- Split-screen mode: Use the split-screen mode to use Trello alongside other apps at the same time, e.g. B. to take notes or access resources.

- Touchscreen functions: Tablets allow for convenient touchscreen operation. Use drag-and-drop functions to move cards around, or swipe to mark tasks as complete.
- Team collaboration: share your tablet with colleagues at meetings or workshops to work together on projects.

A notice: Using Trello on different devices gives you the flexibility to stay productive no matter where you are. The desktop version offers a comprehensive view, while the mobile app is ideal for on the go and tablets offer a comfortable in-between size. Adapt the use of Trello to each platform to make the most of its features and increase the efficiency of your project management.

Protection of data and privacy

Protecting data and privacy is crucial, especially if you use Trello for business or personal purposes. Here are in-depth tips on how to keep your data safe and private in Trello:

1. Password security:

- Use a strong and unique password for your Trello account. A secure password should consist of a combination of upper and lower case letters, numbers and special characters.
- Update your password regularly and never share it with other people.

2. Access Rights and Permissions:

- Use access rights and permissions in Trello to ensure only authorized users can access specific boards or cards.
- Regularly check access rights and remove unnecessary users from shared boards.

3. Sensitive Information:

- Avoid storing sensitive or confidential information in Trello, such as B. Passwords, credit card information or personal data.
- If you need to store sensitive information, use the encrypted text feature in Trello or use a secure password manager application.

4. Use of Business Class or Enterprise accounts:

- If you use Trello for business, consider using Business Class or Enterprise accounts. These offer advanced security features such as single sign-on (SSO), tightened access controls and data transfer via SSL.

5. Archiving and Deletion:

- Archive or delete cards and boards that are no longer needed to reduce the amount of data and remove unnecessary information.
- Note that archiving cards and boards still allows access to the information they contain. If you want to permanently delete data, check the deletion features in your account or contact Trello Support.

6. Public Boards:

- Be careful when creating public boards as they can be viewed by anyone. If you share sensitive information, make sure you set up access controls accordingly.

7. Updates and security patches:

- Keep your Trello app, operating system, and browser up to date to benefit from the latest security patches and updates.

8. Security in integrations:

- If you use third-party integrations, make sure they are trustworthy and keep your data safe.

A notice: Protecting data and privacy in Trello requires proactive measures and regular reviews. By following the tips and best practices above, you can minimize the risk of data leakage or unauthorized access. Remember that Trello's security depends not only on the platform itself, but also on your behavior and settings. Be careful when using Trello for sensitive information and follow security best practices to protect privacy.

Account security recommendations

Account security is critical to protecting your data and privacy in Trello. Here are detailed recommendations on how to keep your Trello account safe:

1. Use a strong and unique password:

- Choose a password that is a combination of uppercase and lowercase letters, numbers, and special characters. Avoid easy-to-guess passwords like "123456" or "password".
- Use a separate password for Trello that you don't use for any other accounts. This prevents compromising one account from compromising other accounts as well.

2. Enable two-factor authentication (2FA):

- Enable two-factor authentication in your Trello account. This adds an extra security factor, ensuring that even if someone knows your password, only you have access to your account.
- You can set up 2FA with an authenticator app like Google Authenticator or with SMS codes.

3. Check and manage your access rights:

- Regularly check the access rights and permissions for your boards and cards. Remove users or team permissions that are no longer needed.
- Make sure only trusted people have access to sensitive or confidential information.

4. Watch out for phishing attempts:

- Be wary of emails asking you to log in to a Trello-like site. Always check the URL and be alert to suspicious emails that might be phishing attempts.
- Never enter your password or login credentials on a suspicious website.

5. Use secure networks:

- Use public WiFi networks with caution as they can be insecure. Avoid logging into your Trello account from public computers or devices.
- Always use a secure internet connection when accessing your Trello account.

6. Keep your device and software up to date:

- Make sure you're always using the latest version of the Trello app, operating system, and browser.
- Keep your apps and software updated to take advantage of the latest security patches and features.

7. Don't share sensitive information in Trello:

- Avoid storing sensitive information like passwords, credit card information, or personally identifiable information in Trello.
- Instead, use secure password management applications for sensitive information.

8. Monitor your account activity:

- Check your Trello account activity regularly to spot any unusual activity or suspicious logins.

- Report suspicious activity to Trello Support immediately.

A notice: Account security is an ongoing process. By following the recommendations above and making sure you follow security best practices, you can significantly improve the security of your Trello account. Be proactive and protect your credentials and data from unauthorized access to ensure the highest level of privacy and security.

case studies
and
Application examples

How companies use Trello for different projects

Businesses can use Trello for a variety of projects and tasks because the platform is flexible and adaptable. Here are detailed examples of how companies use Trello for different projects:

1. Project management: Trello is great for project management. Businesses can create boards for individual projects and use lists to track the different phases of the project, such as: B. "In planning",

"In progress", "Completed". Cards represent individual tasks that team members can add, comment on, and move to track progress.

2. Product development: For new product development, companies can use Trello to collect ideas, prioritize features, and track development status. Trello makes it possible to collect feedback and requirements from customers and organize the development process efficiently.

3. The marketing campaign: Trello can be used for planning and executing marketing campaigns. Businesses can create boards to manage various marketing projects such as: B. Social media campaigns, advertising measures or event planning. Lists can represent each phase of the campaign, and cards provide details about each task.

4. Event management: For event and event organization, Trello can be used to manage all aspects such as: B. Planning, budgeting, venue, speakers, logistics and attendee registration. Each event can have its own board, and cards can include details about each task and activity.

5. Personnel management and recruiting: Trello can be helpful in managing human resources and the recruiting process. Companies can create boards for open positions, create lists for the recruitment process and use cards for individual applicants to track the entire application process.

6. Customer care and support: Trello can be used to manage the customer care process and support team. Organizations can map customer requests, assign ownership, and track status to ensure all requests are processed in a timely manner.

7. Project overview and reporting: Businesses can also use Trello as a project dashboard to get an overall view of ongoing projects and tasks. By linking all relevant boards together or using power-ups, they can have a clear view of progress and performance in real-time.

A notice: Trello's versatility allows companies to use the platform for different projects and tasks. The customizability of the boards, lists, and cards allows teams to organize and streamline their workflows, regardless of the type of project. Trello encourages transparency, collaboration, and productivity, making it a valuable tool for companies looking to successfully manage their projects.

Successful project management scenarios

Successful project management is the key to achieving goals and successfully implementing projects. Here are detailed scenarios where Trello is successfully used as a project management tool in different situations:

1. **Software development:** In a software development project, Trello can be used to organize the development process. The board can represent the different phases of the project, such as: B. "Requirements Analysis", "Development", "Testing" and "Release". Lists can represent the various functions or modules to be developed in the software. The cards can then represent the individual tasks and bugs, which are assigned the appropriate responsibilities, due dates, and priorities. The development team can drag the cards through the lists to track the development progress.

2. Marketing campaign: In a marketing campaign project, Trello can be used to manage the entire campaign process. The board can represent the different phases of the project, such as: B. "Planning", "Implementation", "Monitoring" and "Analysis". Lists can represent the different activities of the campaign, such as: B. "Social Media Posts", "Email Marketing" and "Content Creation". The cards can then include the individual tasks, planned release dates, and the team members involved. The marketing team can drag the cards through the lists to track campaign progress and ensure all activities are completed on time.

3. Event management: In an event management project, Trello can be used to manage all aspects of the event. The board can represent the different phases of the project, such as: B. "Planning", "Logistics", "Sponsor acquisition" and "Execution". Lists can represent the different aspects of the event, such as: B. Venue, Programming, Attendee Registration, and Marketing. The cards can then contain the individual tasks, responsibilities and due dates. The events team can swipe the cards through the lists to follow the progress of the event and ensure everything is running smoothly.

4. Product development: In a product development project, Trello can be used to brainstorm ideas, prioritize features, and track the development process. The board can represent the different phases of the project, such as "idea generation", "requirements analysis", "development" and "release". Lists can represent the different functions or modules to be developed in the product. The cards can then contain the individual features or ideas, which are assigned the appropriate responsibilities and priorities. The development team can drag the cards through the lists to track development progress and ensure all features are implemented on time.

5. Customer Care and Support: In a customer care or support project, Trello can be used to manage customer requests and organize the support process. The board can represent the different stages of the support process, such as: B. "Open Requests", "In Progress", "Resolved" and "Closed". Lists can represent the different types of requests, such as B. "Technical Support", "Returns and Exchanges" and "Product Information". The cards can then contain the individual requests with the appropriate details, responsibilities and due dates. The support team can swipe the cards through the lists to track the progress of the case and ensure that all customer requests are dealt with appropriately and in a timely manner.

A notice: Trello's flexibility and customizability make it an effective tool for various project management scenarios. No matter the type of project, Trello can help organize tasks, track progress, improve communication, and ensure projects are completed efficiently. The above examples are just a few of the many ways companies can successfully use Trello to make their projects a success.

Summary

Trello is a versatile and flexible project management tool that companies can use successfully in different scenarios. It enables effective organization, tracking and collaboration in various projects and tasks.

In software development, Trello can be used to structure the development process, tracking phases like requirements analysis, development, and testing, and assigning responsibilities and due dates to tasks.

In marketing, Trello is ideal for planning and implementing campaigns. Different lists represent activities like social media posts or email marketing, and cards contain tasks with scheduled release dates and team members.

For event management, Trello can manage all aspects of the event, from planning to execution. Lists can represent event logistics, program planning, and attendee registration, while cards contain individual tasks and responsibilities.

In product development, Trello makes it possible to collect ideas, prioritize features, and track development progress. Lists can represent different modules or functions, and cards contain individual features with responsibilities and priorities.

In the area of customer care and support, Trello helps to manage customer requests and the support process. The board can represent stages such as "Open Requests" and "Resolved," while lists represent different types of requests. The cards include details, responsibilities, and due dates for each request.

To keep Trello accounts secure, use strong and unique passwords and enable two-factor authentication. Sensitive information should be avoided and access rights checked regularly.

In summary, Trello offers the ability to efficiently organize projects, track progress, and improve collaboration. Its adaptability allows it to be used in various fields such as software development, marketing, event management, product development and customer support. By using Trello, companies can optimize their project management processes and successfully achieve their goals.